The World Since 1945

6TH EDITION

THE WORLD SINCE 1945

A History of International Relations

WAYNE C. MCWILLIAMS
HARRY PIOTROWSKI

LYNNE
RIENNER
PUBLISHERS

BOULDER
LONDON

Published in the United States of America in 2005 by
Lynne Rienner Publishers, Inc.
1800 30th Street, Boulder, Colorado 80301
www.rienner.com

and in the United Kingdom by
Lynne Rienner Publishers, Inc.
3 Henrietta Street, Covent Garden, London WC2E 8LU

Library of Congress Cataloging-in-Publication Data
McWilliams, Wayne C.
The world since 1945 : a history of international relations /
    Wayne C. McWilliams, Harry Piotrowski.— 6th ed.
    Includes bibliographical references and index.
    ISBN 1-58826-347-9 (pbk. : alk. paper)
    1. World politics—1945–1989. 2. World politics—1989–
3. Military history, Modern—20th century. 4. Developing countries.
I. Piotrowski, Harry. II. Title.
D840.M363   2005
327'.09'045—dc22   2005000400

British Cataloguing in Publication Data
A Cataloguing in Publication record for this book
is available from the British Library.

Printed and bound in the United States of America

        The paper used in this publication meets the requirements
 ∞   of the American National Standard for Permanence of
        Paper for Printed Library Materials Z39.48-1992.

    5 4 3 2 1

In Memoriam

Bill Sladek
1938–1993

friend and colleague

■ Contents

■ Illustrations

■ MAPS

■ PHOTOGRAPHS

The World Since 1945